Who Wa Frank Lloyd Wright?

Who Was
Frank Lloyd Wright?

by Ellen Labrecque

illustrated by Ted Hammond

Penguin Workshop

For Sam and Juliet—EL

To my mom—TH

PENGUIN WORKSHOP
An Imprint of Penguin Random House LLC, New York

Text copyright © 2015 by Ellen Labrecque.
Illustrations copyright © 2015 by Penguin Random House LLC. All rights reserved.
Published by Penguin Workshop, an imprint of Penguin Random House LLC, New York.
PENGUIN and PENGUIN WORKSHOP are trademarks of Penguin Books Ltd.
WHO HQ & Design is a registered trademark of Penguin Random House LLC.
Printed in the USA.

Visit us online at www.penguinrandomhouse.com.

Library of Congress Control Number: 2015040467

ISBN 9780448483139   10 9 8 7

Contents

Who Was
Frank Lloyd Wright?

For Frank Lincoln Wright's ninth birthday, his mother, Anna Lloyd Jones, bought him a special set of building blocks. The wooden blocks came in many shapes and sizes: cubes, spheres, and pyramids. There were shiny papers to cover them, and sticks to connect them.

On that day in 1876, Anna dreamed her son would grow up to be a famous architect. An architect is a person who designs buildings such as homes, schools, hospitals, and museums. An architect plans what a building will look like inside and out. He also makes sure it is built safely.

Frank loved his new toys and played with them all day long. He learned how shapes fit together. And he learned that he could make bigger and bigger structures by putting smaller shapes together in the right order.

During Frank's long life, he designed more than 1,100 buildings, including small houses, giant mansions, churches, temples, office buildings, and even a world-famous museum. When asked how he could create so many new projects, Frank answered, "I can't get them out fast enough." He could barely keep up with his own ideas!

Frank's ideas led to some of the most creative structures ever built. He designed a house in Pennsylvania called Fallingwater that sits on top of a waterfall! He constructed an office building in Wisconsin that has columns shaped like giant lily pads at the top. He designed the Guggenheim art museum in New York City—a building that looks like a giant teacup from the outside. Inside, a spiral ramp rises toward a domed skylight.

In 1991, the American Institute of Architects declared Frank "the greatest American architect of all time." He really did become one of the world's best architects. And Frank's journey all began with a set of blocks!

Chapter 1
Mother Knows Best

Frank Lincoln Wright was born June 8, 1867, in Richland Center, Wisconsin. His middle name was a tribute to Abraham Lincoln, who had died two years earlier. Frank's father, William Carey Wright, was a preacher and a musician.

William Wright already had three other children—Charles William, George Irving, and Elizabeth Amelia—with his first wife, who had died a few years earlier. William married Anna in 1866.

Frank's mother, Anna Lloyd Jones, had ten brothers and sisters. Her family had moved to rural Wisconsin from the country of Wales.

Her father—Frank's grandfather, Richard Jones—
had been a preacher in Wales. He wanted more
freedom to preach as well as more land to farm.
But when the family moved to Wisconsin, there
were no houses to buy. Instead the Jones family
had to build their own. This role fell to Anna's
oldest brother, Thomas.

Thomas taught himself how to design and
build a home for his own family.

At the time, many people were moving to the area and buying farmland. They needed somebody to build their houses for them. Thomas's skills were soon in demand. Anna decided that if she ever had a son, she wanted him to have the same useful skills as her brother.

With that in mind, Anna hung drawings of English cathedrals—large, fancy churches—on the walls of their home when Frank was a baby. She wanted to inspire his young brain!

During Frank's childhood years, William moved his family all over the country looking for work. He worked as a music teacher and as a pastor for different churches. The family lived in

Iowa, Rhode Island, and Massachusetts, all before Frank was ten years old. By then Frank had two more sisters—Jane and Margaret Ellen, who was called Maginel.

William only made a small salary as a preacher and a teacher. He usually had many debts to pay. The large family never seemed to have enough food and clothes for everybody.

Frank did not have the same interests as his sisters, so he often played alone. And it was hard to make friends with neighborhood boys because Frank's family moved around so much. He turned to art and music to fill his days. These were things he could enjoy on his own. He spent hours drawing with colored pencils and learning to play the viola and the piano.

Frank's mother adored him. She was convinced he would grow up to be a great and famous man. Frank began to believe this about himself, too.

Even though money was tight, Frank's mother still saved enough to buy her son Froebel blocks for his ninth birthday. The blocks helped teach Frank about geometry, math, colors, and shapes.

The constant moving and money troubles were very difficult for the Wright family. In 1878, the family moved to Madison, Wisconsin, where Anna would be near her brothers and sisters for help and support. Her family welcomed them back home.

FRIEDRICH FROEBEL
(1782—1852)

BORN IN GERMANY, FRIEDRICH FROEBEL BECAME A TEACHER IN HIS EARLY TWENTIES. HE BELIEVED HIS STUDENTS SHOULD LEARN BY PLAYING, NOT BY SITTING AT DESKS AND LISTENING TO GROWNUPS TALK.

IN 1837, FRIEDRICH FOUNDED THE FIRST KINDERGARTEN FOR CHILDREN AGES THREE TO SIX YEARS OLD. THE GERMAN WORD *KINDERGARTEN* MEANS "CHILDREN'S GARDEN." FRIEDRICH DESCRIBED HIS SCHOOL AS A TRAINING GROUND FOR LITTLE CHILDREN.

FRIEDRICH'S IDEAS ABOUT EARLY EDUCATION INSPIRED HIM TO DESIGN A SERIES OF WOODEN TOYS CALLED FROEBEL BLOCKS. THE BLOCKS ARE SPHERES, CYLINDERS, CUBES, AND PYRAMIDS. FROEBEL BLOCKS ARE STILL SOLD TODAY, NEARLY 180 YEARS AFTER THEY WERE INVENTED!

Chapter 2
The School Years

Back in Wisconsin, Frank spent his summers working on his uncle James's farm.

It was forty miles away from the Wrights' new home in Madison. He had to get up at four in the morning to milk the cows. After a big breakfast, Frank fed the pigs and calf, and then did farm work.

Frank didn't like the hard work. He cried
all the time, and even tried to run away twice.
Frank's mother's family had a motto: "Adding
tired to tired and then adding it again." This
meant Frank was supposed to keep working, no
matter how tired he became!

Frank didn't hate every moment on the farm, though. He loved looking at the beautiful hills and valleys nearby. He loved all the colors and shapes he found in nature. Frank saw the shapes of his boyhood toys everywhere on the farm. He saw a long triangle in each carrot, a square in each of the corn kernels, and circles in some stones and rocks. He started to think of the giant trees as different types of beautiful buildings.

"From sunrise to sunset there can be nothing so beautiful in any garden as in these wild Wisconsin pastures," he later wrote.

Frank spent five summers on the farm, returning to Madison to go to school each fall. By then he was sixteen years old, and the hard work had made him confident and strong. He believed that he could do anything if he was willing to work hard for it.

One day, Frank watched as workers rebuilt the dome of the Wisconsin State Capitol Building. Suddenly, the dome collapsed. A cloud of dust rose into the air. Most of the workers were killed.

The building contractor was to blame. He had ordered the workers to use inferior materials to construct the columns. The loss of life caused by this error in judgment horrified Frank.

The accident had a big impact on young Frank. He promised to make sure every building he designed was physically sound and safe.

Family life remained difficult in the Wright household. Frank's mother and father fought all the time.

William still struggled to make enough money to support his family. He had opened a music school when he and his family moved to Madison. But he never made enough money to make the school a success. Eventually, he had to shut it down.

In April 1885, William and Anna got divorced. William left his wife and children the house. Frank never saw his father again. Shortly thereafter, eighteen-year-old Frank changed his middle name from Lincoln to Lloyd in honor of his mother's side of the family.

Once his father left, Frank's family had even less money. To help support them, Frank dropped out of Madison High School. He had always been just an average student. He didn't like to sit still and listen to teachers. Frank liked to learn by exploring, creating, and doing things on his own.

Frank got a part-time job working as a
junior draftsman for an architectural firm. An
architectural firm is a company hired by other
businesses to design and build buildings. As a
draftsman, Frank had to draw plans that would be
used as the instructions for making buildings.

Frank had no experience or formal training as a
draftsman. He had never taken art lessons, and he
did not know how to create building plans. But his
mother convinced his new bosses he was a natural

artist, a quick learner, and a hard worker. All these things were true.

At the same time, Frank enrolled at the University of Wisconsin at Madison. He was considered a "special student," because he did not have a high-school diploma. One of the architects he worked for was also a professor there. The university did not have an architectural school. But it did have a school for civil engineering, the next-best thing to architecture in Frank's mind.

ARCHITECTURE VS. CIVIL ENGINEERING

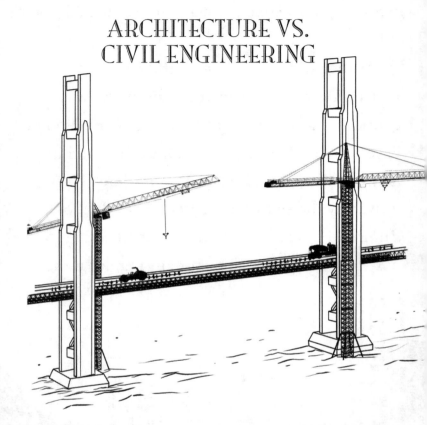

AN ARCHITECT AND A CIVIL ENGINEER HAVE A LOT IN COMMON. BOTH DESIGN AND BUILD STRUCTURES. BUT THEIR JOBS HAVE DIFFERENCES, TOO.

ARCHITECTS DESIGN AND BUILD MANY TYPES OF BUILDINGS, INCLUDING OFFICES, LIBRARIES, MUSEUMS, AND HOMES. ARCHITECTS WANT THEIR BUILDINGS TO BE SAFE AND WELL-BUILT.

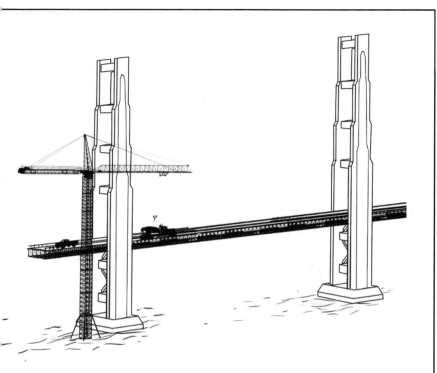

BUT THEY ALSO STUDY ART AND DESIGN. THEY
WORK HARD TO CREATE BEAUTIFUL BUILDINGS
THAT PEOPLE WILL WANT TO LOOK AT AND LIVE
OR WORK IN.

CIVIL ENGINEERS BUILD PUBLIC BUILDINGS
AS WELL AS ROADWAYS, CANALS, AND BRIDGES.
THEY ALSO FOCUS ON STRENGTH AND SAFETY.
BUT THEY ARE LESS INTERESTED IN THE WAY
A BUILDING LOOKS. THEIR GOAL IS TO MAKE
STRUCTURES BETTER AND MORE EFFICIENT
FOR ALL THE PEOPLE WHO WILL USE THEM.

As a draftsman, Frank was paid thirty-five dollars a month and even played a small role in designing the university's new science center. In the morning, he took classes in French, mathematics, English, and engineering. He worked in the afternoon, then had his evenings free to study.

Frank used some of the money he earned from his job to buy fancy clothes. He often wore a top hat and fancy shoes with pointed toes. He carried a cane when he walked across campus. He wasn't a famous architect yet, but he wanted to look like one.

Chapter 3
Blossoming Architect

Frank had been at the University of Wisconsin for less than a year when he dropped out. He had decided to move to Chicago, Illinois. Because the Great Chicago Fire of 1871 had destroyed many of the city's downtown buildings, many architects had moved there to help rebuild the city. Frank wanted to go to Chicago and learn from the best.

On a spring afternoon in 1887, Frank boarded a train for Chicago. He arrived with big dreams but just seven dollars in his pocket.

THE GREAT CHICAGO FIRE

THE GREAT CHICAGO FIRE IS THE MOST WELL-KNOWN FIRE IN THE HISTORY OF THE UNITED STATES. ON OCTOBER 8, 1871, A FIRE BROKE OUT IN A BARN ON THE CITY'S WEST SIDE. TO THIS DAY, NO ONE KNOWS HOW THE FIRE STARTED, BUT IT WAS OUT OF CONTROL WITHIN MINUTES.

HELP ARRIVED TOO LATE, AND SEVERAL BLOCKS HAD ALREADY BURNED DOWN. THE FIRE BURNED FOR TWO DAYS, UNTIL EARLY OCTOBER 10, WHEN IT WAS FINALLY PUT OUT. BY THEN, IT HAD DESTROYED MUCH OF THE CITY.

THE FIRE TOOK THREE HUNDRED LIVES AND DESTROYED 17,450—MOSTLY WOODEN—BUILDINGS. ABOUT ONE-THIRD OF THE CITY WAS BURNED TO THE GROUND, AND NEARLY ONE HUNDRED THOUSAND PEOPLE WERE LEFT HOMELESS.

A well-known architect and family friend, J. L. Silsbee, worked in Chicago, and Frank went to ask him for a job. In 1885, Mr. Silsbee had designed a church for Frank's mother's family—the Lloyd Joneses—in Wisconsin.

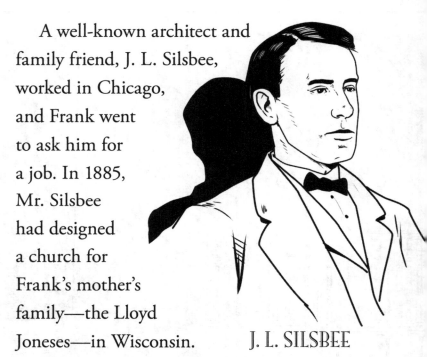

J. L. SILSBEE

Mr. Silsbee was designing a new church in Chicago, and one of Frank's uncles, Jenkin Lloyd Jones, happened to be the preacher there.

Mr. Silsbee offered Frank a job that paid eight dollars a week. Because Frank had little experience, he just did tracing—copying somebody else's drawings. Frank spent hours watching Mr. Silsbee draw, hoping to improve his own skills.

Eventually, Frank proved to be a natural with a pencil in his hand. Mr. Silsbee named him one of his draftsmen.

One of Frank's first jobs was for his own family. He designed a school building for two of his aunts, who had started the Hillside Home School on the family's farmland back in Wisconsin.

After working for Mr. Silsbee for one year, Frank heard there was a draftsman job open at a different company. Dankmar Adler and Louis Sullivan were rising stars in the business, and Frank wanted to work for the best. He also wanted to make more money.

Frank marched over to their office and showed Mr. Sullivan, the company's top architect, his drawings. Mr. Sullivan was impressed with Frank's enthusiasm and hired him on the spot. He was paid twenty-five dollars a week, a big raise from his job with Mr. Silsbee.

Frank's mother, Anna, and his youngest sister, Maginel, had followed him to Chicago and now lived with him. Frank's half brothers and sisters were all grown and living on their own. His other sister, Jane, was now a teacher.

Frank worked tirelessly day and night. He became better and better at drawing. His ideas were new and different. Mr. Sullivan saw how talented Frank was. After just a few short years, he offered Frank a raise and put him in charge of thirty other draftsmen.

Both Frank and Mr. Sullivan believed America needed its own style of architecture. Up until the late 1870s, a lot of the buildings in America had been copies of buildings in Europe. Many homes were designed in a Victorian style that had originated in England.

Frank, who grew up in a simple, gray wooden home, thought Victorian-style houses looked like big, ugly, cluttered boxes. To him, small rooms with too much stuff in them felt like jail cells.

Frank preferred houses with open spaces, few walls, and little clutter. On the outside, Frank wanted his homes to blend in with the shapes and the colors already found in nature. Nobody had ever thought about designing houses this way before. Most people were happy to have showy-looking homes that stood out.

VICTORIAN-STYLE HOUSES

VICTORIAN-STYLE HOUSES FIRST APPEARED DURING THE REIGN OF QUEEN VICTORIA OF ENGLAND (1837–1901). IN THE UNITED STATES THIS STYLE WAS MOST POPULAR BETWEEN 1860 AND 1900. VICTORIAN-STYLE HOUSES, SOMETIMES CALLED "PAINTED LADIES," OFTEN LOOKED LIKE GINGERBREAD HOUSES WITH BRIGHTLY-COLORED TRIMMINGS AND LARGE PORCHES OUTSIDE.

INSIDE, THESE HOMES WERE DIVIDED INTO MANY DIFFERENT ROOMS FILLED WITH FURNITURE, ART, LAMPS, RUGS, AND ALL SORTS OF COLLECTIONS. A BARE OR SIMPLE ROOM IN A PLAIN HOUSE WAS NOT CONSIDERED FASHIONABLE DURING THE VICTORIAN ERA.

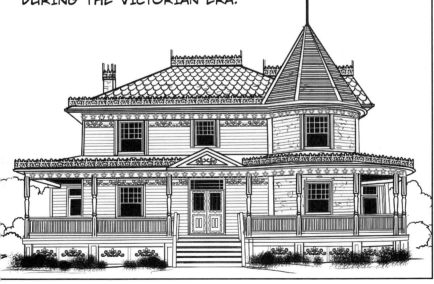

Now that Frank was successful, he grew even more confident. As he got older, he discovered he loved to talk with people. He had grown to be a charming, handsome young man, with dark wavy hair and piercing eyes.

In 1887, he attended a costume party at his church and met Catherine Lee Tobin, who was called Kitty. Kitty was just sixteen years old and beautiful. She came from a wealthy Chicago family. Frank and Kitty fell in love right away.

After Frank and Kitty got married, Frank asked his boss, Mr. Sullivan, for a loan. He wanted to use the money to build his first home. Mr. Sullivan agreed. Frank bought land outside Chicago in a neighborhood called Oak Park.

Frank gave the house that was already on the property to his mother and sister. Then he built a new home next door for himself and Kitty. The young couple married on June 1, 1889, shortly after Kitty turned eighteen. Their first child,

Frank Lloyd, was born the following year. Their second child, John Lloyd, was born in 1892.

Kitty spent her time looking after the boys. Frank spent his time building his career.

Chapter 4
On His Own

Over the next few years, Frank designed many homes for wealthy people in the area. All the homes were simple and uncluttered. They blended into the land that surrounded them. And they didn't look anything like the older homes that stood near them. People began to talk about Frank's houses. He called his style "organic architecture."

WHAT IS ORGANIC ARCHITECTURE?

ORGANIC ARCHITECTURE IS A WAY OF CONSTRUCTING HOUSES OR OTHER BUILDINGS SO THAT THEY BLEND IN WITH THEIR NATURAL SETTING. STRUCTURES CREATED IN THIS MANNER ARE USUALLY PAINTED IN EARTHY COLORS LIKE BROWNS, GREENS, AND REDS.

INSIDE, THE BUILDING IS DESIGNED SIMPLY, WITH JUST A FEW WALLS, MINIMAL FURNITURE, AND PLENTY OF OPEN SPACE. HOMES BUILT IN THE ORGANIC STYLE HAVE MANY WINDOWS SO THAT SUNLIGHT CAN FILL THE ROOMS. THE LIGHT MAKES SPACES SEEM EVEN LARGER. MORE WINDOWS ALSO ALLOW PEOPLE TO EXPERIENCE THE LAND, TREES, WATER, AND NATURAL SCENES THAT SURROUND THEIR HOMES.

"THE GOOD BUILDING MAKES THE LANDSCAPE MORE BEAUTIFUL THAN IT WAS BEFORE THE BUILDING WAS BUILT," FRANK SAID. IN OTHER WORDS, A HOUSE DESIGNED ORGANICALLY CAN ACTUALLY IMPROVE THE LOOK OF THE PROPERTY IT SITS ON.

Frank's organic designs were soon in demand all around the Chicago area. In 1893, he left Adler and Sullivan to work on his own.

People loved Frank's new design style, but they were also drawn to Frank himself. He and Kitty loved to host and attend parties. He had a laugh that was contagious, and he loved to talk and tell funny stories.

He wore a hat with a wide brim and sometimes even slung a dramatic cape over his shoulders. And whenever he had the chance, Frank discussed his ideas about organic architecture. He was able to attract a lot of new clients because he was so outgoing.

Between 1893 and 1901, Frank designed
seventy-one new buildings. Most of his work
was for private homes in the Chicago area.
Frank also built a studio—his workroom—

next to his own house. But instead of cutting
down a willow tree that stood in the way, Frank
built a hallway around the tree to connect the
studio to his home. The tree trunk was indoors,
and the top branches stuck right out of the roof!

Frank and Kitty also continued to have more children. By 1903, they had a total of six: four sons and two daughters. Frank built a playroom on the top floor of the house. In the playroom, the Wright children played with Froebel blocks, just like their father had when he was a boy.

Frank's children each played an instrument as soon as they were old enough to learn. Frank wanted to put a piano in the playroom, but he didn't want the big instrument to get in the way of the children's play area. So he cut a space into one of the walls. The back of the piano was hidden behind the wall, and only the keyboard remained on the playroom side! Frank was a master at keeping spaces uncluttered!

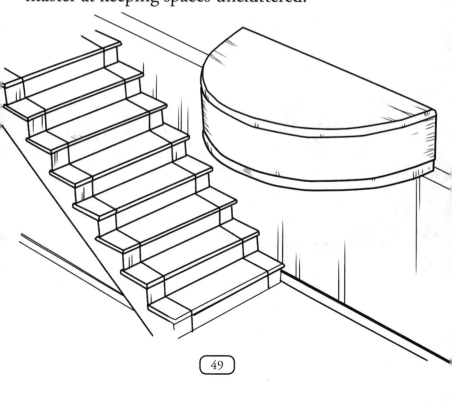

Because Frank was so convinced that homes should match the land they were built on, he developed a new look. It was called "prairie style." Prairie-style homes were built to blend in with the flat prairie land of the Midwest. They were built low to the ground, were usually two stories high, and did not have attics or basements. They also had lots of windows and usually a large fireplace in the center.

Frank always thought of the Froebel blocks from his childhood when he built new homes. One house even had a stained-glass window filled with the blocks' geometric shapes.

Frank's designs continued to win fans. But he wasn't well known outside the United States, or even much outside the Chicago area. Frank wanted to be famous all over the world, and knew he had to take on bigger projects to make this happen.

In 1903, Frank designed his first major public work—something other than a private home.

It was an office building for the Larkin Mail
Order Company in Buffalo, New York.

Like his prairie houses, the building was
designed with lots of windows to allow more
natural light into the office space. On the first
floor, all the secretaries worked together in an
open, cheerful space. The managers—bosses of
the company—sat in office balconies overlooking
them. Frank also created fireproof metal furniture
and the first complete air-conditioning unit to

keep the workers cool. Nobody had ever designed an office building like this before. The Larkin building was a huge success and became the talk of the architecture world.

Chapter 5
The Japan Years

While he was building his career as an architect, Frank had spent most of his time working. Kitty raised the children on her own. Frank and Kitty were no longer close. He had met a woman named Mamah Borthwick Cheney while designing a house for her and her husband.

Frank fell in love with Mamah. He asked Kitty for a divorce, but she said no.

A German publisher named Ernst Wasmuth offered to create a book about Frank's work. Frank wanted to go to Germany to work with Ernst. And just like his own father had years earlier, Frank left his family. He took Mamah with him. In Germany, he gathered all the drawings, photographs, and floor plans of the buildings he had designed. The book, known as the "Wasmuth portfolio," was a huge hit.

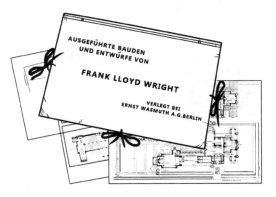

It was published in 1910 and made Frank famous all over the world. He was forty-three years old and had been designing buildings for twenty years.

Frank and Mamah stayed in Europe for over a year. When Frank returned to the United States, he did not live with Kitty and his children. Frank's mother gave him thirty-one acres of her family's land in Spring Green, Wisconsin. And Frank moved there with Mamah. He built a home called Taliesin, a Welsh word meaning "radiant."

Frank designed their house to look as though it had grown out of the side of a hill. It had lots of windows where Frank could look out over the valley where he had spent time farming as a boy.

Frank and Mamah lived at Taliesin for three years. On August 14, 1914, tragedy struck. A handyman named Julian Carlton burned the house down. The fire killed Mamah, her two children, and four workers. Julian Carlton survived the fire.

But when it was discovered that he had set the fire on purpose, he was caught and put in jail. Frank was away at the time, working in Chicago.

Frank was heartsick over what had happened, but he worked through his grief. "In action," he said, "there is release from anguish of mind."

Over the next six years, Frank worked to rebuild Taliesin. He was also busy designing the Imperial Hotel. The hotel was being built in Tokyo for the emperor of Japan.

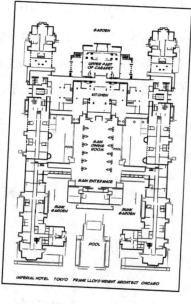

Frank knew that Japan had been hit by many earthquakes. He needed to build the Imperial so it could withstand one. He didn't want his work to collapse like the Wisconsin State Capitol Building had so many years ago.

Frank designed the hotel so it wouldn't fall over easily in an earthquake. He built the walls thicker at the bottom than at the top. This made the building more stable. He also built the hotel in sections, like train cars. This way, if one section toppled, it wouldn't pull the whole building down with it.

Frank worked on the hotel from 1917 to 1922. Frank's second oldest son, John Lloyd, worked as his assistant.

Watching the hotel being built gave John Lloyd, now an architect himself, an idea for a new toy. John Lloyd thought kids could create their own toy buildings if they had the right materials. With this in mind, John Lloyd invented Lincoln Logs.

The Imperial Hotel opened in 1922. That same year Frank and Kitty were finally divorced.

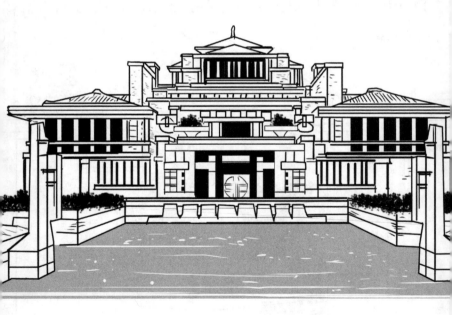

LINCOLN LOGS

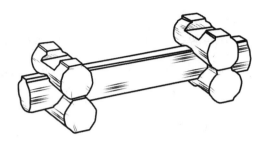

JOHN LLOYD WRIGHT INVENTED LINCOLN LOGS IN 1916. HE NAMED THE POPULAR TOY AFTER PRESIDENT ABRAHAM LINCOLN, WHO WAS BORN IN A LOG CABIN.

THE ORIGINAL LINCOLN LOGS WERE MADE OF REDWOOD AND CAME IN DIFFERENT LENGTHS AND SIZES. THE LOGS HAD NOTCHES ON EACH END SO THAT THEY COULD EASILY FIT TOGETHER.

BY COMBINING DIFFERENT-SIZE LOGS WITH DOORS, WINDOWS, AND BLOCKS, CHILDREN COULD BUILD THEIR OWN CABINS, FORTS, AND HOUSES. SINCE LINCOLN LOGS WERE INVENTED, MORE THAN ONE HUNDRED MILLION SETS HAVE BEEN SOLD AROUND THE WORLD.

IN 1999, LINCOLN LOGS WERE INDUCTED INTO THE NATIONAL TOY HALL OF FAME.

For the many years they had been living apart, Kitty had held out hope that Frank would return to her and their children. But that never happened. Frank had visited his children and they had visited him, but he was never a traditional father. He once said that he never had the "father feeling" for his children, he only had it for his buildings.

Frank felt in order to achieve his goal of becoming a world-class architect, he had to put his work before his family. Frank was a great artist and builder. But he was also a selfish man at times.

On September 1, 1923, the day of the Imperial Hotel's completion ceremony, the great Kanto earthquake shook Japan. It was one of the most powerful earthquakes in Japan's history. More than 140,000 people died, and 300,000 buildings were destroyed. Frank's hotel was one of the few buildings that were still standing after the quake.

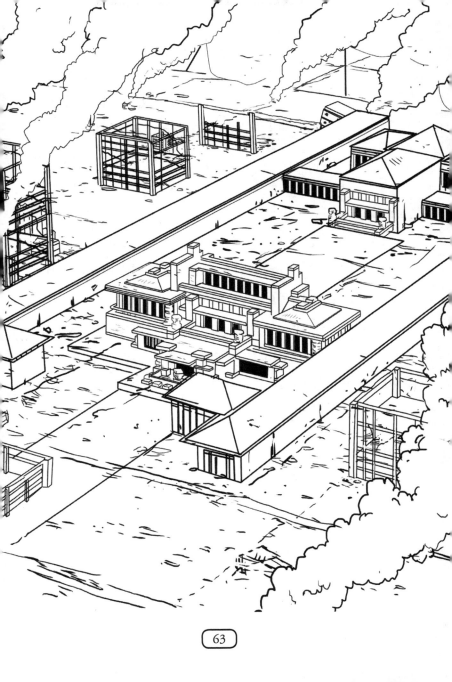

Frank was back in the United States when

the earthquake hit. A few days later he received a telegram from a representative for the emperor of Japan. The telegram said: "Hotel stands undamaged as monument to your genius. Congratulations!" Frank framed this telegram and hung it on the wall in his office. The fact that his hotel survived the earthquake, while so many other buildings collapsed, made Frank and his work more famous than ever.

Chapter 6
The Tough Years

Despite Frank's success with the Imperial Hotel, he did very little building over the next ten years. Frank always believed his designs were the best, and he didn't like to compromise. If a builder asked him to change a detail on a building, he sometimes got mad and refused to do it.

Sometimes his projects were canceled because Frank's design cost more money than the builder intended to spend. And occasionally, Frank was even fired so that another architect could design the building instead.

It was a sad time in Frank's personal life as well. His mother, who had been his biggest supporter throughout his life, died in 1923. Then in 1925, Taliesin caught fire again and was badly damaged, though no one was hurt this time. Frank worked hard to rebuild the house once more.

Frank married an artist and sculptor named Maude Miriam Noel, in 1923. But they were divorced just four years later. In 1928, Frank married Olgivanna "Olga" Hinzenberg. Olga was a great beauty and thirty-three years younger than Frank. Together they had a daughter, named Iovanna.

With his new family, Frank's personal life

became much steadier. But Frank's career suffered even more. One reason was the Great Depression.

During the Depression, most people didn't have the money to build new homes. The world of architecture was changing. Designers were moving away from creating buildings with wood and stone, and began working with glass and metal instead.

THE GREAT DEPRESSION BEGAN ON OCTOBER 29, 1929, WHEN THE NEW YORK STOCK MARKET CRASHED. THAT MEANT THAT MANY PEOPLE WHO INVESTED THEIR MONEY IN STOCKS—SHARES OF OWNERSHIP IN COMPANIES—LOST THEIR LIFE'S SAVINGS. BUSINESSES, FACTORIES, AND STORES ALL SHUT DOWN. EVEN BANKS CLOSED.

BY 1933, ONE OF EVERY FOUR PEOPLE IN THE UNITED STATES WAS OUT OF WORK. A DROUGHT IN THE GREAT PLAINS STATES MADE THE SITUATION EVEN WORSE. FARMERS COULD NOT GROW ENOUGH CROPS. FOOD BECAME SCARCE.

THE GREAT DEPRESSION DIDN'T REALLY END IN THE UNITED STATES UNTIL THE COUNTRY ENTERED WORLD WAR II IN 1941. FACTORIES BEGAN TO PRODUCE WEAPONS, AIRPLANES, SHIPS, AND OTHER PRODUCTS NECESSARY FOR THE WAR EFFORT. THE ECONOMY BEGAN TO RECOVER WITH NEW JOBS, AND THE COUNTRY FOUND A RENEWED PURPOSE.

Modern technology allowed architects to design cheaper houses and other buildings. These structures were built quickly and at the same time by construction crews. They often looked the same.

Just as Frank didn't like Victorian architecture, he didn't like mass-produced buildings. Right after the stock market crashed, he said that just because people lived in the machine age, it didn't mean their houses should look like machines built them.

With few opportunities to construct new
buildings, Frank began to lecture at colleges and
universities around the country. He also wrote a

book about his early life
and his opinions on art,
architecture, and even
love. It was called *An
Autobiography*.

Still, without more
work, Frank needed to
make more money. He
came up with an idea.

In 1932, with the help of his wife, Olga, Frank
opened a school on the land next to Taliesin.

He called the school the Taliesin Fellowship, and up to sixty students came each year to work and learn under him. The students studied design and other arts such as sculpture, painting, dance, and music. They also did farm work such as chopping wood and growing their own food, just like Frank did when he was a boy.

One student at the Fellowship was Edgar Kaufmann Jr. Edgar's father owned a famous department store in Pittsburgh, Pennsylvania. The Kaufmanns also owned two thousand acres of land in a beautiful, wooded area south of the city. The Kaufmanns wanted to build a house near a waterfall on their land, and Mr. Kaufmann asked

Frank to design it. Frank thought about what he wanted to build for nine months. When he sat down to draw the house, he completed the plans in two hours!

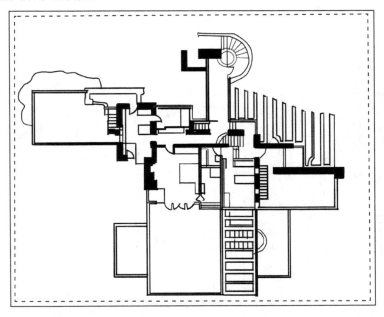

Instead of designing a house *near* the waterfall, Frank designed a house that was built right *on* the rocky ledge of the waterfall! The house seemed to grow right out of the rock. Every bedroom had a balcony that hung right over the waterfall.

The balconies looked like diving boards hanging above a swimming pool. Frank named the house Fallingwater. When the house was completed in 1937, other architects and builders saw it as a masterpiece.

Articles about the stunning house appeared in newspapers and magazines all over the country. Frank even appeared on the cover of *TIME* magazine.

Fallingwater's success turned things around for Frank. His work was now back in demand. Frank was seventy years old. But instead of retiring, he entered the most creative and successful period of his career.

Chapter 7
Famous Again

Now that Frank was the most famous architect in America, many wealthy people wanted him to design expensive homes for them. Herbert Jacobs, a journalist, wrote to Frank asking if he would consider designing an inexpensive house for his family in Madison, Wisconsin. Mr. Jacobs only wanted to spend $5,000. In comparison, Fallingwater had cost $155,000 to build.

Frank loved the new challenge.

He wanted to see if he could design an affordable but stylish home for ordinary people according to his vision of organic architecture.

The Jacobses' house was built between 1936 and 1937. Frank called it a "Usonian house." "Usonian" was a word Frank made up. It meant the house was developed for people living in the United States. He hoped the whole country would follow this style of design.

The Jacobses' house was a small, single-story, flat-roof structure that did not have a basement or attic. He used natural materials such as local wood, stone, and baked clay to build it.

The house was bright and open, with plenty of windows and few walls. It did not have a lot of closets. Frank did not believe in storing clutter. To save even more money, Frank buried the hot-water pipes under the floor to heat the entire house.

The Jacobses loved this stylish, tiny, and affordable home. So did many other people. Strangers knocked on the Jacobses' door every day asking for tours. More and more middle-class people around the country asked Frank to design houses for them, too. More than one hundred Usonian houses were built over the next twenty years.

In 1937, Frank designed another unique house, this one for Paul Robert Hanna and his wife, Jean. The house was called the Hanna Honeycomb House. It was

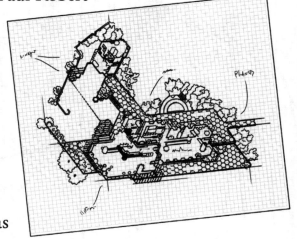

built on the campus of Stanford University in Palo Alto, California, where Paul Hanna taught.

The design was the first one Frank ever created that was not rectangular. He designed the house based on the six-sided hexagon shapes that make up the tiny chambers inside a honeycomb (the wax cells that bees build to store their honey). Rather than four right angles, every room had six obtuse angles. Everything in the house—the tables and even the beds—had the shape of a hexagon or part of a hexagon. The Hanna family even kept honeybee hives in their backyard.

Other people soon began asking Frank to design buildings that were "outside the box," or different from anything that had been done before. Herbert Johnson, the president of the Johnson Wax Company, asked Frank to create an office building that was so beautiful, workers would rather stay at work than go home. This was another challenge Frank had no trouble accepting. During the years he spent constructing the Usonian houses, he designed the new Johnson Wax office building in Racine, Wisconsin.

When it was finished in 1939, the structure
was just as sleek and elegant as Mr. Johnson had
hoped it would be. Frank had designed gorgeous
columns that looked like giant lily pads. These lily
pads supported the ceiling of the main workroom.

Each column was only nine inches at the bottom, and spread out until it became eighteen feet wide at the top. Light streamed in through a narrow band at the top of the walls. The building truly was a work of art. Mr. Johnson began offering tea to employees after work because they actually *did* want to stay!

During this time, Frank still lived at Taliesin and ran the Fellowship school, but he was tired of the harsh Wisconsin winters. He bought land in the Arizona desert and built another home and school, which he called Taliesin West.

Frank designed this structure to match the surrounding desert, using sand and rocks he found locally.

Frank was so busy building his new home and school that he didn't even stop to pay attention to world news. When

Frank and his students heard that the United States had entered World War II in December 1941, they just kept on working.

"It was like living on the moon," explained one of Frank's students at Taliesin West. "We never read the newspaper or even listened to the radio while we were there."

Throughout the war, from 1939 to 1945, Frank, his family, and his students spent half the year at Taliesin and half the year at Taliesin West.

Frank worked all the time, sometimes even
straight through the night. He was busy designing
new buildings for Florida Southern College
in Lakeland, Florida. The president of Florida
Southern told Frank he wanted to transform
his small college into a national showplace.

Frank eventually designed eighteen new buildings for the college campus. Twelve of them were actually built.

Chapter 8
Working to the End

The years between 1946 and 1959 were the most productive years of Frank's life. He created 260 new designs, including a glass temple in Pennsylvania that looked like a mountain, and a gas station in Minnesota with an observation tower. He designed a Unitarian church in Wisconsin that looked like two hands folded together in prayer.

One of his last and most famous designs was the Guggenheim Museum in New York City.

In 1943, Solomon Guggenheim, a businessman and art collector, hired Frank to build a new art museum. Mr. Guggenheim wanted a museum that looked completely different from all others. Frank, seventy-six at the time, welcomed this challenge. He was so excited, he told Mr. Guggenheim, "I am so full of ideas for our museum that I am likely to blow up . . . unless I can let them out on paper."

SOLOMON GUGGENHEIM (1861–1949)

SOLOMON GUGGENHEIM WAS BORN INTO A
WEALTHY FAMILY IN PHILADELPHIA, PENNSYLVANIA.
IN THE LATE 1800S, HE BEGAN COLLECTING ART.
AND BY 1919 HE WAS COLLECTING ART FULL-TIME.

IN 1937, SOLOMON SET UP THE SOLOMON R. GUGGENHEIM FOUNDATION. THE FOUNDATION'S MISSION IS TO "PROMOTE THE UNDERSTANDING AND APPRECIATION OF ART." IN OTHER WORDS, TO ENCOURAGE ALL PEOPLE—NOT JUST THE WEALTHY—TO LOOK AT ART AND GROW TO LOVE IT THE WAY SOLOMON HAD.

BY THE EARLY 1940S, SOLOMON NEEDED A PERMANENT PLACE TO DISPLAY HIS ART COLLECTION. THAT'S WHEN HE ASKED FRANK LLOYD WRIGHT TO DESIGN A NEW MUSEUM. SOLOMON GUGGENHEIM DIED ON NOVEMBER 3, 1949, TEN YEARS BEFORE THE SOLOMON R. GUGGENHEIM MUSEUM OPENED IN NEW YORK CITY.

Frank wanted to create a museum that would be as interesting as the art hanging on the walls. He designed a building that looks like a giant teacup. Inside, a ramp spirals to the top of the building. An elevator takes visitors to the top of the ramp so they can slowly make their way down and view the museum's collection of great art.

It took sixteen years to get the Guggenheim Museum built. This was in part because so many people opposed what Frank designed. Many thought its odd, swirling shape would look strange amid the other buildings nearby. Artists thought the building itself would take people's attention away from the art on display. One newspaper article even called Frank Lloyd Wright "Frank Lloyd Wrong." But Frank always believed in his designs. He thought the shape of the space would complement the paintings hanging there.

On April 9, 1959, Frank died in his sleep at Taliesin West, at the age of ninety-one. This was just six months before the Solomon R. Guggenheim Museum was finished.

When the museum opened its doors, visitors
flocked to see Frank's one-of-a-kind building.
The design was eventually considered to be
a remarkable work of art.

One critic called the finished museum "positive and overpowering."

Frank was buried near Taliesin in Wisconsin, only a few feet from his mother's grave. He had made her dreams and his own come true.

He became one of the greatest architects who ever lived. He created buildings that nobody imagined possible. He changed the way people used the land, lived in their homes, and worked in their offices. Nature had been Frank's biggest influence. And he believed his respect for nature was the key to his success.

The Frank Lloyd Wright Foundation—founded by Frank in 1940—is still going strong today. The Foundation oversees the School of Architecture at Taliesin and Taliesin West, and maintains both of Frank's homes, one located at each site.

FRANK LLOYD WRIGHT ON NATURE

- I BELIEVE IN GOD, ONLY I SPELL IT NATURE.

- STUDY NATURE, STAY CLOSE TO NATURE. IT WILL NEVER FAIL YOU.

- BUILDINGS, TOO, ARE CHILDREN OF EARTH AND SUN.

- NO HOUSE SHOULD EVER BE ON A HILL OR ON ANYTHING. IT SHOULD BE OF THE HILL. BELONGING TO IT. HILL AND HOUSE SHOULD LIVE TOGETHER, EACH THE HAPPIER FOR THE OTHER.

Frank's papers, designs, and drawings are preserved at these locations. So is his vision of organic architecture.

Until the day he died, Frank always felt that he had more designs in his future, that he could always keep working. Whenever asked which building was his greatest, Frank always responded, "The next one."

TIMELINE OF FRANK LLOYD WRIGHT'S LIFE

1867	Frank Lincoln Wright is born on June 8
1885	Enrolls at the University of Wisconsin, Madison; Changes middle name from Lincoln to Lloyd
1887	Starts working as a draftsman for the Chicago architect Joseph L. Silsbee
1888	Works for Adler and Sullivan, one of the most important architectural firms in Chicago
1889	Marries Catherine Lee "Kitty" Tobin on June 1
1893	Opens own practice in Chicago
1911	Begins building Taliesin in Spring Green, Wisconsin
1914	Taliesin burns down
1916	Builds the Imperial Hotel in Tokyo, Japan
1922	Divorces Kitty
1928	Marries Olgivanna Hinzenberg on August 25
1932	Publishes *An Autobiography* Opens the Taliesin Fellowship as a school for architects
1937	Builds Fallingwater and the first Usonian house Begins building Taliesin West in Scottsdale, Arizona
1943	Begins designing the Solomon R. Guggenheim Museum in New York City
1959	Dies in Arizona on April 9
1991	The American Institute of Architects names Frank Lloyd Wright "the greatest American architect of all time"

TIMELINE OF THE WORLD

United States buys Alaska from Russia — **1867**

Thomas Edison invents the first practical lightbulb — **1879**

The Statue of Liberty, France's gift to the United States, is erected — **1886**

World's Fair held in Chicago, Illinois — **1893**

Theodore Roosevelt becomes the twenty-sixth president of the United States — **1901**

Wilbur and Orville Wright carry out the first steered motor flight — **1903**

Earthquake destroys much of San Francisco — **1906**

World War I begins — **1914**

World War I ends — **1918**

American Charles Lindbergh is first to complete a solo, nonstop flight over the Atlantic Ocean — **1927**

Franklin Delano Roosevelt becomes president of the United States
Adolf Hitler becomes chancellor of Germany — **1933**

World War II begins — **1939**

World War II ends — **1945**

Led by Martin Luther King Jr., African Americans begin a 381-day bus boycott in Montgomery, Alabama — **1955**

BIBLIOGRAPHY

* Adkins, Jan. **Frank Lloyd Wright: A Twentieth-Century Life**. New York: Puffin, 2008.

Huxtable, Ada Louise. **Frank Lloyd Wright: A Life**. New York: Lipper/Viking, 2004.

Kann, Bob. **Frank Lloyd Wright and His New American Architecture**. Madison: Wisconsin Historical Society Press, 2010.

* Levy, Janey. **The Architecture of Frank Lloyd Wright: Understanding the Concepts of Parallel and Perpendicular**. New York: Rosen, 2005.

Secrest, Meryle. **Frank Lloyd Wright**. New York: Knopf, 1992.

*Books for young readers

* Thorne-Thomsen, Kathleen. **Frank Lloyd Wright For Kids: His Life and Ideas.** Chicago: Chicago Review Press, 1994.

Wright, Frank Lloyd. **An Autobiography**. New York: Duell, Sloan and Pearce, 1943.

WEBSITES

www.franklloydwright.org

www.fallingwater.org